FAMILY TIES

PAIRED:

A son and a daughter searching for their roots.
To understand himself, Barack Obama had to discover
the truth about his dead father. Amy Tan found her
voice as a writer by telling the story of her mother's past.

"Away from my mother, away from my grandparents, I was engaged in a fitful interior struggle. I was trying to raise myself to be a black man in America, and . . . no one around me seemed to know exactly what that meant."

Barack Obama

"When my feet touched China, I became
Chinese. I knew I was not totally Chinese,
but I felt the connection nevertheless. It was
a sense of completeness, like having a mother
and a father. I had China and America, and
everything was all coming together finally."

Amy Tan

Photographs © 2012: Alamy Images: 62 (Bon Appetit), 94 (Photos 12); Alexander Warnow: 100; AP Images: 46 (Darko Bandic), 54, 56 (Ron Edmonds), 23 (Kyodo), 24 (Obama for America), 12, 14, 18, 32 (Obama Presidential Campaign), back cover right, 3 right (Joe Tabacca), 99 (Michael C. York); Corbis Images/Bettmann: 44; Everett Collection, Inc.: 69, 84; Getty Images: 82 (AFP), 10 (Robert Harding), 30 (Laura S. L. Kong), 50 (Saul Loeb/AFP), 49 (Peter Macdiarmid), back cover left, 3 left (Jim Watson/AFP); Jim McHugh: 60, 70; Media Bakery: cover bottom, cover top; NEWSCOM/Jacob Wire/Rapport Press: 38; Courtesy of Oakland Public Library, Oakland History Room: 65; ShutterStock, Inc./Vladimir Mucibabic: 73; The Granger Collection, New York: 86; The Image Works: 58 (Bildarchiv Monheim/akg-images), 90 (Albert Harlingue/Roger-Viollet), 78 (Zheng Xianzhang/Panorama).

Library of Congress Cataloging-in-Publication Data

Bahadur, Gaiutra, 1975-
Family ties / Gaiutra Bahadur.
p. cm. -- (On the record)
Includes bibliographical references and index.
ISBN-13: 978-0-531-22554-7 (pbk.)
ISBN-10: 0-531-22554-2
1. Obama, Barack--Family--Juvenile literature. 2. Tan,
Amy--Family--Juvenile literature. 3. Obama, Barack H. (Barack Hussein),
1936-1982--Juvenile literature. 4. Tan, Daisy--Juvenile literature. 5.
United States--Biography. I. Title.
E909.B34 2012
973.932092--dc22
2011016605

Tod Olson, Series Editor
Marie O'Neill, Creative Director
Curriculum Concepts International, Production

Copyright © 2012 Scholastic Inc.

10 11 12 13   40   21 20 19 18

FAMILY TIES

Sometimes you have to travel to find your way home.

Gaiutra Bahadur

Contents

A FATHER'S SECRETS

As a mixed-race kid growing up with his white mother and grandparents, Barack Obama wondered where he fit in. His search took him to Africa, looking for the father he never knew.

Barack Obama, age 17, celebrates his graduation from high school in Hawaii in June 1979. With him are his grandparents Madelyn and Stanley Dunham, who raised him for many years.

1

In Black and White

Barack Obama spent much of his youth under the caring eyes of his grandparents. He and his mother, Ann Dunham, lived on and off with her parents, Madelyn and Stanley Dunham.

Obama, whose father was a black man from Kenya, had darker skin than his white grandparents. But that had never really mattered to him. He called them Gramps and Toot—short for "Tutu," the Hawaiian term for grandmother. They called him "Barry," as everyone did when he was young.

Barack Obama plays on a beach in Hawaii with
his grandfather Stanley Dunham in the 1960s. The
Dunhams were originally from Kansas and moved
to Hawaii after World War II.

One morning Barry woke to the sound of the Dunhams arguing. He went out to investigate and discovered that Toot was upset. She'd wanted her husband to drive her to work that morning. Usually she took the bus. But the day before, a panhandler had cornered her at the bus stop and asked for money. She had given the man a dollar, but he had blocked her way and frightened her. Now Toot was afraid to return to the bus stop. Gramps, for some reason, was insisting that she go.

"Why don't you just let me give her a ride?" Barry asked. "She seems pretty upset."

"She's been bothered by men before," Gramps replied. "You know why she's scared this time? I'll tell you why. Before you came in, she told me the fella was *black*.

That's the real reason why she's bothered. And I just don't think that's right."

Barry felt like someone had punched him in the gut. He steadied himself and told his grandfather that it bothered him too, but that Toot would get over it soon enough. Gramps, looking defeated, apologized for mentioning it to Barry and left to drive his wife to work.

Left alone, Barry sat on his bed thinking. He had been raised by white people, but most Americans would say he looked black. He'd been reminded of it plenty of times. A kid in grade school once hooted like a monkey when the teacher asked what African tribe Barry's dad belonged to. Another kid asked whether his father was a cannibal. And Barry had punched a boy in the nose for calling him a "coon."

But when the outside world felt hostile, his loving family had always provided a refuge. The idea that his kind grandmother could fear a man because of his dark skin left Barry confused and hurt. "That was a powerful moment for me," he later recalled. "Even within families with the best intentions, race can intrude in ugly ways."

Barack Obama would spend the next decade trying to figure out what role race played in his life. How could he be "black" when he'd been raised in a white environment? What did terms like "black" and "white" even mean for a mixed-race kid like himself?

These questions would send Obama on a journey to discover the father he had never gotten to know.

This photograph from the 1960s shows Obama with his mother, Ann Dunham. "She was a very strong person," Obama said in an interview. "Resilient, able to bounce back from setbacks, persistent."

2
Beginnings

Barack Obama's father and mother met in a class at the University of Hawaii. Barack Hussein Obama Sr. was a 24-year-old international student from a small Kenyan village. Ann Dunham was a 17-year-old white woman from Wichita, Kansas.

Obama and Dunham decided to get married in early 1961. It wasn't a simple decision. At the time, interracial marriage was a serious crime in 22 states. But Hawaii wasn't one of them, and the young couple was able to wed.

Barack Obama Jr. was born in Honolulu later that year, but his father had left by his first birthday. Obama Sr. accepted a scholarship to study at Harvard University in Cambridge, Massachusetts. His wife decided not to follow him. They divorced in 1964, and after graduating from Harvard, Obama Sr. returned to Kenya.

Barry's adventures, however, were just beginning. In 1965 his mother married Lolo Soetoro. He was a graduate student from Indonesia, a nation of islands in the South Pacific. Barry was six years old when he and his mother joined Soetoro in Jakarta, Indonesia's capital.

Barry attended school in Jakarta and adjusted quickly to his new life. Two small crocodiles and an ape named Tata lived in his backyard. He ate roasted grasshoppers and snakes. He learned the Indonesian language while playing with new friends in the neighborhood. He welcomed a half sister, Maya, to the family.

As Barry grew up, his mother tried to help him connect to his black heritage. She gave him records by the gospel singer Mahalia Jackson. She had him listen to the civil rights speeches of Martin Luther King Jr.

To be black was something to be proud of, she told him. And Barry's father was her favorite example. She described him as someone who had grown up poor but had achieved great things through hard work, intelligence, and integrity. He had been the first African to attend the University of Hawaii. He won top honors as a straight-A student and went on to study at Harvard.

He returned to Kenya to become one of the country's bright young leaders.

After Barry finished fourth grade, his mom sent him back to Hawaii to continue his schooling. He lived with his grandparents and earned a spot at Punahou, a top private school in Honolulu.

Before the year was over, he would finally meet his father.

In 1972 Barack "Barry" Obama was in sixth grade at Punahou School in Hawaii. He's standing in the back row, second from the left.

When Barack Obama was ten years old, his father visited him in Hawaii. Obama hadn't seen his father for eight years, and after the visit, he never saw him again.

3

Belonging

Barry Obama was confused. The man who stood before him in his grandparents' apartment looked nothing like the man Barry had imagined.

Barry had memorized his father's face from photos his mother had shown him. The man in those pictures was tall, handsome, and confident, with coal-black skin.

But the man who stood in front of him now was so thin that Barry could see the bones of his knees. He walked with a cane and a slight limp, the result of a car accident in Kenya. Obama Sr. crouched to hug his son. "Well, Barry," he said. "It's a good thing to see you after so long. Very good."

It was December 1971. Barry's mother was visiting from Indonesia. His father had come to see him for the first time in nearly a decade. To prepare for the visit, Barry had done some research about his father's people, the Luo. What he learned disappointed him. The Luo lived in mud huts. They herded goats and ate some kind of grain called millet. The men wore small loincloths around their waists.

When Barry's teacher invited Obama Sr. to speak to their class, Barry feared the worst. He had told all kinds of lies to his classmates. He insisted that his father was a Luo prince. Obama meant "Burning Spear," he claimed. He was sure his dad's real story would embarrass him.

But Obama Sr. impressed the fifth graders and teachers at Punahou School. His British accent came out in a rich rumble. He captured everyone's imagination with tales of Kenya's people and wildlife.

For one brief month Barry's father was part of his life. He gave his son a basketball. He took him to a jazz concert. He taught him how to swivel his hips when he danced. But he also scolded the son he barely knew for watching too much TV and not studying harder. He was pushy and self-centered. He got into arguments with Barry's mother and grandparents. Then he was gone.

Obama felt abandoned—just when he needed a father to guide him. Gramps was a good man. But he couldn't help his grandson work through what it meant to be a black man.

As Barry moved through his teens, his need to know how to "be black" grew more pressing. He tried to learn through pop culture and books. He practiced dance steps from *Soul Train*—a TV show that featured black pop stars like Aretha Franklin and The Jackson 5. He copied the slang of comedian Richard Pryor. He read black authors like Malcolm X, James Baldwin, and Ralph Ellison.

Basketball offered the easiest doorway into the world of black men. Barry tried to master the behind-the-back passes and slashing drives of basketball superstar

Julius Erving. But "playing black," with all the fancy moves, was discouraged at school. His coach favored a more controlled style of play.

Barry sometimes played pickup games with black soldiers from nearby military bases. He joined in their banter and copied their way of speaking. He would agree when they said things like "That's just how white folks will do you."

Still, that kind of bitterness did not feel right. "I would find myself talking . . . about white folks this or white folks that, and I would suddenly remember my mother's smile," he recalled in his memoir. How could he condemn all white people when they included his family?

Barry had a handful of black classmates and friends at Punahou. They talked about the

Barack Obama rises for a shot for the Punahou varsity basketball team in 1979. One high school coach says Obama never went anywhere without the basketball that his father had given him. "I remember him bouncing his ball, books in one hand, ball in the other hand."

challenges of growing up in an environment with few black people. They discussed dating non-black girls and the pros and cons of "acting white" or "acting black."

Once Barry told one of his closest friends, Keith Kakugawa, that maybe they should give the angry black man pose a rest. Like Barry, Keith was biracial—black and Japanese. After all, Barry said, they were at the best private high school in Hawaii. They weren't trapped in the ghetto or facing daily discrimination.

"A pose, huh?" Keith shot back. "Speak for your own self."

But for Barry, that was part of his struggle. He still wasn't sure who his "own self" was.

Obama sits in New York City's Central Park. After high school, Obama enrolled at Occidental College in Los Angeles. There he was a troubled and indifferent student. He transferred to Columbia University in New York City his junior year and decided to "buckle down and get serious."

4
Rocking Barack

After graduating from Punahou in 1979, Obama enrolled at Occidental College in Los Angeles. In his easygoing style, he moved between groups—blacks, whites, Asians, Arabs. He joined the school's Black Students Association but was not a very active member.

One of his black friends at Occidental, Eric Moore, had worked in a medical clinic in Kenya, near where Obama's father had been born. According to journalist

David Remnick, Moore remembers asking Obama, "What kind of name is 'Barry' for a brother?" When Obama told him his real name, Moore was impressed. "That's a very strong name. I would embrace that," he said. "I would rock Barack."

After two years at Occidental, Obama transferred to Columbia University in New York City. "I was concerned with urban issues, and I wanted to be around more black folks in big cities," he reflected later. He decided to take Moore's advice and discard "Barry" in favor of "Barack."

Around this time, Obama and his father exchanged letters. Obama Sr. was glad to hear from his son and invited him to visit Kenya. "The important thing," Obama's father wrote, "is that you know your own people, and also that you know where you belong."

In November 1982, not long after receiving the invitation, Obama got a phone call from an aunt in Kenya. His father had died in a car accident. "At the time of his death," Obama wrote, "my father remained a myth to me, both more and less than a man."

Obama sent a letter of condolence to his relatives in Kenya. But he had not known his father well enough to feel much pain or loss. He moved on with his life.

After graduating, Obama decided not to follow those classmates who were headed to graduate school. In June 1985 he moved to Chicago to take a job as a community organizer.

Obama settled in a diverse part of the city, Hyde Park. His apartment was a short elevated-train ride from his job on

Chicago's mostly black South Side. There he helped poor families campaign to improve services and housing in the neighborhood. He worked seven-day weeks, often from sunrise to sundown.

As he burrowed into his work, Obama enjoyed being part of an African American community. His dedication to his work made him welcome. And he took satisfaction in helping people take control of their lives.

In 1987 Obama got a visit from his half sister Auma. She had been born in Kenya and was now doing graduate work in Germany. The two hit it off and talked for hours about their lives, present and past. Auma shared stories about their father—the "Old Man," she called him. She told Obama that their father had struggled painfully after he returned to Kenya. He had become a bitter and broken man.

Obama was stunned. For so long he had imagined his absent father as a brilliant scholar, an ambitious leader, and a great man. Now a much more complex and sad picture was emerging.

Before she left, Auma repeated their father's invitation to come to Kenya. This time, Obama was ready to make the journey and fill in his incomplete picture of his father.

Obama sits with Sarah Onyango Obama (in blue) and other relatives in Kogelo, Kenya. Obama wrote that in Kenya he "began to imagine an unchanging rhythm of days . . . where you could wake up each morning and know that all was as it had been yesterday."

5
His Father's Place

The airline attendant asked him, "You wouldn't be related to Dr. Obama, by any chance?"

"Well, yes—he was my father," Obama replied.

Barack Obama Jr. had just arrived at the Jomo Kenyatta Airport in Kenya. He was pleasantly surprised that the woman had recognized his name. It made him feel at home. This was a land where his name sounded normal and his family had roots.

It was the summer of 1988, one year after Auma's invitation. Obama had recently left his job in Chicago. He would be starting law school at Harvard University in the fall. In the meantime, he had finally come to see his father's homeland.

Auma gave him a tour of Nairobi, Kenya's capital. She introduced him to half brothers, uncles, cousins, and aunts, who smothered him with affection. He suddenly had a huge family to welcome him.

Auma took Obama to the family compound in Kogelo, a village near the shores of Lake Victoria. Obama's father had grown up there, surrounded by goats, chickens, and cornfields. He had also been buried there, in the family cemetery.

In Kogelo, Obama met Sarah Onyango Obama, his father's stepmother. As Sarah braided Auma's hair in the shade of a mango tree, Obama sat down beside them on a straw mat. He asked Sarah about his family's history. In the storytelling tradition of the Luo, she shared a tale that reached back generations. She started with Hussein Onyango Obama—her husband and Barack Obama Sr.'s father.

In the early 1900s, when Onyango was young, a rumor reached his family: white men carrying guns had shown up in a nearby village. The elders of Onyango's village warned their people to stay away from the strangers. But Onyango ignored the warnings and went to meet them. He came back months later dressed in strange clothes. His brothers laughed at his trousers and shirt. Onyango's father was so angry that he told his son to leave and never return.

The white men who so fascinated Onyango were colonists from Great Britain. The British were seizing territory across East Africa. They forced Africans off the most fertile land to start their own farms and coffee plantations. They made the Luo and other groups pay taxes. They pressed Africans into service building railroads, laboring on white-owned farms, and fighting in their army.

Onyango became a servant for the British soldiers and colonists. He cooked for them, adopted their manners, and was paid in their money. He learned to read and write English. He became a wealthy farmer, well respected in his village. He was hot tempered and often cruel, but also generous to those less fortunate than himself.

In the 1940s, conflict between Kenyans and their British rulers disrupted Onyango's privileged life. Resistance to the British was growing all across East Africa. Many Kenyans were determined to drive out the colonists who had stolen their land. Nationalist groups met in secret to plan a rebellion against colonial rule.

In 1949 Onyango was suspected of joining one of the rebel groups. He was thrown into prison and frequently beaten. When the British released him six months later, he could barely walk.

At the time of Onyango's arrest, his eldest son was a teenager. Barack Obama Sr. excelled in school and grew into a young man with a promising future. In 1959 he won a golden opportunity. Kenya was on the brink of independence from Great

British police hold suspected Kenyan rebels at gunpoint in 1952. Thirty-two colonists were killed during the rebellion, which the British ruthlessly suppressed. As many as 90,000 Africans were killed, and thousands more were tortured.

Britain. To prepare for the transition, Kenyan leaders sent their best and brightest young adults to colleges overseas. Obama Sr. earned a spot in the program. He was expected to return with the expertise to help govern the new country.

Barack Obama Sr. returned to Kenya with degrees from the University of Hawaii and Harvard, having left Ann Dunham and Barack Jr. behind in the United States. He became an economist in Kenya's independent government. But he wasn't happy about the way the new leaders ran the country. He criticized officials for taking bribes and complained when unqualified people were given jobs simply because of their political connections.

Kenya's first president, Jomo Kenyatta, summoned Obama Sr. to his office and

This 1987 photograph shows Barack Obama and his stepgrandmother Sarah Onyango Obama. It hangs in her home in the village of Kogelo, in western Kenya.

ordered him to stop causing trouble. Obama Sr. refused to listen and was eventually fired.

Obama Sr.'s career and personal life began a downward spiral. He lost job after job. Failures and disappointments piled up. He beat his wives. He drank heavily and got into several car accidents. He was driving drunk the night he was killed.

The more Sarah talked, the better Barack Obama understood his father and his grandfather. Like Obama himself, the two men had been trapped between two worlds. His grandfather had grown up in a traditional African society but tried to make his way among the Europeans. His father had been educated in the U.S. but returned to work in Kenya.

After Sarah finished, Obama wandered over to a mango tree on the compound. Both his grandfather and father lay buried beneath the tree. He could imagine these proud men trying to carve out their places in a changing world.

Obama sat between the graves. He cried for them and for himself. He no longer felt resentful that he had to figure out his place in the world. Hadn't these men, whose blood he shared, faced the same challenge, and against even greater odds?

If his father and grandfather had stumbled, he thought, it was because of their pride. Neither of them had been able to learn from the past or welcome the help of others. They had tried to do it alone.

Obama vowed not to make the same mistake.

When Barack Obama was in Kenya, he visited his
father's grave (foreground) as well as his grandfather's
(background). A plaque on his grandfather's grave
read "HUSSEIN ONYANGO OBAMA, B. 1895. D. 1979."
His father's grave had only a blank space.

President Barack Obama walks alongside daughters Malia (center) and Sasha on the South Lawn of the White House in October 2010. Obama married Michelle Robinson in 1992, and their daughters were born in 1998 and 2001.

6

The Making of a President

Barack Obama Jr. returned to the U.S. with a clear vision for his future. He received his law degree in 1991. After graduating, he returned to Chicago, where he taught constitutional law and organized people to vote. He was elected to the Illinois State Senate in 1996.

His personal life came into focus as well. In 1992 he married Michelle Robinson, a fellow lawyer. They eventually had two daughters, Malia and Sasha. In 1995 he published his memoir, *Dreams from My*

Father. The book recounted his journey to discover the father he never knew and the self he was struggling to find.

When he sat down to write the book, he says, he had a rush of memories. "I remembered the stories that my mother and her parents told me as a child, the stories of a family trying to explain itself . . . I listened to my grandmother, sitting under a mango tree as she braided my sister's hair, describing the father I had never known."

In 2004 Obama told his story again, this time in a speech that introduced him to millions of Americans. He was running for the U.S. Senate, and the Democratic Party had chosen him to give an important speech at its national convention.

"Tonight is a particular honor for me," he began, "because, let's face it, my presence on this stage is pretty unlikely. My father was a foreign student, born and raised in a small village in Kenya. He grew up herding goats, went to school in a tin-roof shack. His father—my grandfather—was a cook, a domestic servant to the British . . ."

Obama continued, "While studying here, my father met my mother. She was born in a town on the other side of the world, in Kansas."

Obama went on to say that, like his family members, Americans come from a variety of backgrounds. They argue about politics, have different faiths, identify with different races, and live at different income levels.

Still, he claimed, even as Americans pursue their individual dreams, they "come together as a single American family: 'E pluribus unum,' out of many, one."

On July 27, 2004, Barack Obama gave the keynote address at the Democratic National Convention in Boston. He was elected to the U.S. Senate the following November.

Toward the end of the speech, Obama reflected: "I stand here knowing that my story is part of the larger American story, that I owe a debt to all who came before me, and that in no other country on earth is my story even possible." In no other place on earth, he joked, would a "skinny kid with a funny name" have such cause to hope for his future.

Obama easily won his Senate seat with 70 percent of the vote. Four years later he campaigned for the presidency. He traveled the country, telling his personal story again and again, urging Americans to work together.

In November 2008 Barack Obama was elected, becoming the first U.S. president of African descent.

On January 20, 2009, Barack Obama—with his wife, Michelle, at his side—takes the oath of office to become the 44th president of the United States.

Barack Obama

Born:
August 4, 1961, in Honolulu, Hawaii

Grew up:
Honolulu, Hawaii, and Jakarta, Indonesia

Education:
Occidental College, Columbia University, and Harvard Law School

Website:
www.barackobama.com
www.whitehouse.gov

Favorite books:
The Bible
Parting the Water, Taylor Branch
Song of Solomon, Toni Morrison
Tragedies of William Shakespeare
Writings of Abraham Lincoln

Author of:
The Audacity of Hope: Thoughts on Reclaiming the American Dream
Dreams from My Father: A Story of Race and Inheritance
Of Thee I Sing: A Letter to My Daughters

He says:
"When you start writing you are able to discern where you're being false, where you're using clichés, where you're manufacturing emotion that's not really there, or where you're shying away from something that isn't necessarily flattering."

A MOTHER'S GHOSTS

As a teenager, Amy Tan kept her distance from everything Chinese, including her mother. Twenty years later, a journey to China helped reveal tragic family secrets—and turn Tan into one of America's most beloved writers.

Amy Tan walks through Chinatown in San Francisco, California. "It's a luxury being a writer," Tan says, "because all you have to think about is life."

7
Rebellion

When Amy Tan was 14, a white minister and his family came for Christmas Eve dinner with Amy and her Chinese-born parents. Amy had a crush on the minister's son and was painfully aware of her parents' Chinese ways. Her mother was serving a whole fish with its beady eyes intact. Amy was sure the boy thought it was disgusting. Her father burped loudly and explained it was the Chinese way to compliment a cook. Amy wanted to disappear under the table.

In her nonfiction story "Fish Cheeks," Tan uses descriptions of Chinese food to express her early discomfort with her heritage. She describes her mother serving a "slimy rock cod with bulging eyes" and "a plate of squid [that] resembled bicycle tires."

After the family left, Amy's mother produced an early Christmas gift for her humiliated daughter. Amy had been begging for clothes she could be proud to wear to school. Her mother, surprisingly, had listened. She gave Amy a brand-new miniskirt—and a lecture to go with it. "You want to be like American girls on the outside," she said in her broken English. "But inside you must always be Chinese. You must be proud you different. You only shame is be ashame."

Amy brushed her mother's advice aside. Only years later, as she struggled to find her voice as a writer, would the words come back to her. When she finally began to explore her Chinese heritage, she discovered painful secrets hidden in her mother's past. It was a tragic history. For Tan, it became a source of pride and inspiration.

Amy's parents, John and Daisy Tan, came to the United States from China in the late 1940s. They settled in Oakland, California, where Amy was born three years later. Amy stopped speaking her parents' language when she was five. She could understand them when they spoke to her in Chinese, but she responded in English.

Growing up, Amy often had to communicate for her mother. She translated at banks, stores, and doctors' offices. Daisy Tan even had Amy impersonate her on the phone when she had important calls to make.

For the most part, Amy hated having to act as the family's translator. She saw the way people treated her mother when they heard her broken English. Amy could tell

This photograph of a street in Oakland, California, was taken in 1949, around the time that Amy Tan's parents arrived in the city.

they didn't respect her mother, and it made Amy respect her less as well.

As a young girl, Amy spent hours in front of the mirror trying to wish away her Asian features. She tried to reshape her nose by pinching it with clothespins. It was too broad, she thought, too Chinese. It made her look too much like her mother.

Amy's Chinese name, An-Mei, means "blessing from America." But Amy had a hard time seeing her life as a blessing. In her view, American kids enjoyed a lot more freedom than she did. They could date and go to movies. They didn't have to study all the time, like she and her two brothers did.

Daisy Tan was strict and demanding. She expected Amy to become a doctor or a famous pianist. Amy had to practice piano for an hour every day. She lived in the shadow of her mother's stern warnings. Look both ways before you cross the street, her mother would tell her—or you will be crushed flat as a fish. Don't let boys kiss you. "You do," Daisy Tan told her, "you can't stop. Then you have baby. You put baby in garbage. Police find you, put you in jail, then you life over; better just kill youself."

During Amy's childhood, her mother fell into deep depressions that cast a pall over the family. She'd threaten to kill herself when her children defied her. When she grew unhappy, she'd often make the family move to a new house. Amy changed schools 11 times before she got to high school.

Daisy Tan seemed obsessed with death. "She often talked about death as warning, as an unavoidable matter of fact," Amy Tan recalls. Amy sensed that her mother was haunted by something in her past, but Amy didn't know what it was—and as a teenager, she didn't much care. She wanted more than anything to leave her mother's erratic moods and her Chinese ways behind. "I'm not going to have anything to do with anything Chinese when I leave home," Tan recalled thinking. "I'm going to be completely American."

Tan's novel *The Joy Luck Club* was made into a movie. One of the main characters is a girl similar to the young Amy Tan. In this scene, the girl says angrily to her mother: "I wish you wouldn't do that—tell everyone I'm your daughter."

Amy and Daisy Tan walk together in San Francisco. "I was a complete brat," Amy Tan says about herself as a child. "[My mother] once said that patience was her strength—that if she didn't give up on me, she could endure anything."

8

A Promise to Keep

When Amy Tan was 15, a sudden tragedy turned her life upside down. Her older brother, Peter, and her father both died of brain tumors within seven months of each other. Amy missed her father terribly. He was calm and easygoing—the opposite of her mother. He read bedtime stories and did *Reader's Digest* vocabulary quizzes with Amy and her brothers.

After the deaths, Daisy Tan moved Amy and her younger brother, John Jr., to several places in the U.S., and then to the Netherlands and Germany. They eventually settled in Switzerland, where Amy finished high school.

Shared grief did not bring Amy closer to her mother. In Switzerland she rebelled against her mother's strict rules. She started dating and stayed out late. Daisy Tan was enraged. During one particularly intense fight, she held a meat cleaver to Amy's throat.

The battle of wills continued after the family returned to the United States. Amy Tan left the Baptist college her mother had chosen for her. She followed a new boyfriend to college in San Jose, California, and switched her major from pre-med to English. After that, mother and daughter did not speak to each other for six months.

After the death of her husband and son, Daisy Tan
moved the family to Montreux, Switzerland, a town
on Lake Geneva.

Tan found she enjoyed writing and decided to make it her career. She wrote speeches and other materials for salespeople and business executives. She wrote under pen names like "May Brown" to avoid using her Chinese-sounding name. She worked 90-hour weeks and earned a lot of money, enough to buy her mother a house.

But by age 33, Tan's success had given her little joy. She struggled with depression, like her mother. As a distraction, she tried a different kind of writing—short stories. In her fiction, she could explore her own sadness and the often bitter relationship she had with her mother.

In 1985 Tan wrote "End Game," a short story about a Chinese American girl whose mother pressures her to become a chess champion. *Seventeen* magazine published the story the following year. An agent contacted Tan and asked whether she could write more like it. Tan promised her 16 stories about Chinese mothers and their American-born daughters.

As Tan was beginning to write fiction, she received some frightening news about her mother. Daisy Tan had suffered a heart attack. Amy was on vacation in Hawaii when she found out. As she later described in an essay, her hands shook as she dialed the hospital. She recalled the time when her mother had asked, "If I die, what you remember?" Tan had mumbled something in response, clearly hurting her mother's feelings. "I think you know little percent of me," Daisy Tan had said.

As Amy Tan waited for the hospital switchboard to connect her, she accepted that her mother had been right: Amy did know only "little percent" about Daisy Tan. She knew her mother had been married in China before she met Amy's father. She knew her mother had left three daughters behind when she came to the U.S. Beyond that, her mother's past was a mystery.

Right then, Amy Tan made a promise to herself. "If my mother lives, I will get to know her," she vowed. "I will ask her about her past, and this time I'll actually listen . . . I'll even take her to China, and yes, I'll write stories about her."

Her mother's voice came on the line: "Amy-ah?"

"Oh . . . Mom," Tan said. "Are you okay?"

"Yes, fine, fine. Where you?"

"Hawaii."

"Hawai-hee? When you go Hawai-hee?"

Daisy Tan was fine. She had been arguing about prices at a fish market when she felt a stabbing pain in her chest. She went to the hospital, but the pain had been caused by stress, not a heart attack. She blamed the episode on the fishmonger, who she claimed had been trying to cheat her.

Amy Tan hung up. She felt relieved. But now she had a promise to keep.

This is Nanjing Road in Shanghai. Amy Tan says of her visit to China: "I wanted to see where [my mother] had lived, I wanted to see the family members who had raised her, the daughters she had left behind. The daughters could have been me, or I could have been them."

9

Daisy Tan's Secrets

In 1987 Amy and Daisy Tan boarded a jet for China. It was Amy Tan's first visit to her parents' homeland. She saw where her mother had lived in Shanghai, an ancient seaside city of more than ten million people. Bicycles shared the road with trucks and men pushing carts. People had to boil water to make it safe to drink. Life in China seemed foreign enough to make Tan realize just how American she was.

"I also discovered how Chinese I was," Tan recalled later. She had always felt like a foreigner in high school history class. None of her family members had fought in the American Civil War or voted for Franklin D. Roosevelt. "It was wonderful going to a country where suddenly the landscape, the geography, the history was relevant."

During the trip Tan met her three Chinese sisters—Lijun, Jindo, and Yuhang. Tan had trouble making herself understood, but she felt an instant bond with them. They smiled the way she did. They all moved their hands in similar ways. Sometimes it was like looking in a mirror.

Daisy Tan, Amy discovered, was just as hard on her Chinese daughters as she was on Amy. She scolded them for serving food that was undercooked and too salty. She hated the way they dressed. She told them all to lose weight. Growing up, Amy had blamed her mother's misunderstandings with people on her bad English. Now it was obvious that her mother argued with everyone, in English and Chinese.

As Tan learned more about China, her appreciation of her mother grew. For 20 years the causes of her mother's depression had remained hidden behind a veil of silence. Now Amy began asking about her mother's past, and Daisy Tan opened up and shared the story of her turbulent life.

Daisy had been movie-star beautiful as a young woman in the 1930s. She had married an army pilot who fought the Kuomintang, the Chinese Nationalist

Communist soldiers stand watch from the top of a tank in Shanghai on June 24, 1949, one week after their army had marched into the city.

Party. During the 1930s and 1940s, the Kuomintang fought a bloody civil war with Chinese communists for control of the country.

Daisy's first husband was no gallant warrior; she called him "that bad man." He abused her and cheated with other women. Once he put a gun to her head. Another time, he refused to take their sick baby to the doctor because he was gambling and didn't want to stop. The baby died. Daisy Tan remembered whispering, "Good for you, little one; you escaped."

Daisy tried to escape, too. She had met a more caring man, John Tan, and tried to run away with him. But she was caught, and her husband had her charged with adultery. She was put on trial and sent to jail.

In this scene from the movie *The Joy Luck Club,* a mother abandons her twin baby girls while fleeing communists during the Chinese civil war. Daisy Tan had been forced to leave her own three daughters in China.

By 1949 the communists were on the verge of winning the civil war. Daisy was freed from jail and left the country to be reunited with John Tan, who had fled to California. But "that bad man" who had fathered her three daughters refused to let the girls go with her. Daisy Tan would not see them again for almost three decades.

Amy Tan returned to the U.S. with new stories spinning in her head. She knew her mother in a way she never had before. In learning the history of her Chinese family, Tan had discovered a past that belonged to her. She was beginning to understand the sadness she had absorbed from her mother. "It was a chance," she reflected later, "to see what was inside of me and my mother."

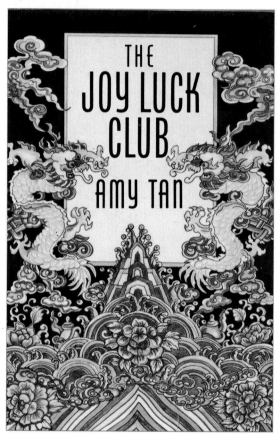

Amy Tan's 1989 book, *The Joy Luck Club,* has sold more than two million copies. It has been translated into more than 30 languages, including Chinese.

10
Ghost Writer

When Amy Tan came home from China, her agent had some remarkable news for her. Tan had only finished three of the 16 stories she had promised to write. Yet publishers were already competing to buy the book.

When she sat down to finish the stories, Tan imagined her mother as the reader. She based the language on the rhythms of her mother's immigrant English and asked her mother to read the early drafts. "So easy to read," Daisy Tan told her daughter.

This compliment made Amy Tan happier than any of the praise she would soon receive from critics.

Tan dedicated the book, *The Joy Luck Club*, to her mother: "You asked me once what I would remember," she wrote. "This, and much more."

The Joy Luck Club was published in 1989, and it changed Tan's life. The book became an instant best seller. It told funny and heartbreaking stories about four Chinese mothers and their daughters. Critics loved it. Hollywood turned it into a movie.

By accident, the book also helped Tan uncover more of her mother's secrets. She knew only a little about her grandmother Jingmei—the woman whose picture hung above the piano while she was growing up.

Jingmei had died of an opium overdose, but Daisy Tan had claimed that it was accidental. In *The Joy Luck Club*, Amy created a tragic character based on her grandmother, but she changed some of the details. The character became a widow who commits suicide after being forced to become a rich man's mistress.

When Daisy Tan read that part of the book, she was startled. Somehow her daughter had stumbled on the truth. Jingmei *had* committed suicide. She had deliberately overdosed on opium after a rich man raped her and made her his concubine (a woman who lives with a man but has a status lower than that of a wife). She killed herself out of shame and misery.

Always superstitious, Daisy Tan thought her mother's ghost had whispered

This 1930 photograph shows two opium smokers.
Opium is a very addictive drug produced from
poppies. Daisy Tan's mother, Jingmei, killed herself
by overdosing on the drug.

the truth to Amy. Hoping to reach Jingmei, Daisy Tan would call out to Amy's computer in Chinese: "Hey, it's me. Are you there? Do you miss me?"

Daisy Tan told her daughter the entire heartbreaking story. Daisy, who was just nine at the time, had been with her mother when she died. At the funeral, monks attached chains to Daisy's ankles. They were supposed to keep the child from flying away with her mother's ghost. But Daisy tried to get free of the chains. She wanted to go with her mother.

Amy Tan found her mother's story a revelation. "The more I heard, the more I wanted to know . . . " she says. "I wanted to go back to the past. I wanted to be there with her, to be her witness, to agree with her, 'Your life was terrible.'"

All the things that drove Tan crazy as a child began to make sense. She realized why her mother had run from house to house as though they were all haunted. Unhappy memories, like ghosts, followed Daisy Tan wherever she went. Amy had inherited sadness from Daisy, just as Daisy had inherited it from her mother. The pain had been passed down from grandmother to mother to daughter.

But Amy Tan was beginning to see this inheritance in a new way. She had the ability, through her writing, to turn the painful history into powerful stories. She could air the family's secrets and give them meaning.

Tan began recording her mother's stories with a video camera. Little by little, she uncovered as many details as she could.

At one point a relative asked Daisy Tan why she shared these stories with her daughter. After all, the relative said, "she can't change the past."

Daisy Tan disagreed. "It can be changed," she said. "I tell her, so she can tell everyone, tell the whole world so they know what my mother suffered. That's how it can be changed."

In this scene from *The Joy Luck Club*, the character based on Daisy Tan is dancing with her husband, who treats her cruelly. As the real Daisy Tan got older, she developed Alzheimer's disease and began to forget many incidents from her painful past.

11

The Blessing of Forgetting

In late 1995 Amy Tan noticed that her mother seemed to be forgetting things. At times she made up memories. She claimed to have been present at events she could only have seen on television.

Tan worried that depression might be causing the memory loss. She asked her mother to see a doctor.

"Nothing wrong with my memory," Daisy Tan responded. "Depress 'cause can *not* forget."

The doctor diagnosed Daisy Tan with Alzheimer's disease, which destroys the brain, and with it, the memory.

Amy Tan was devastated. She couldn't believe that the woman who seemed to remember everything was now losing her past.

Tan had been struggling with her new novel. Its theme was memory. But it was hard for her to think about memory as she watched her mother lose hers.

One day Daisy Tan called, agitated. "I know I did something to hurt you . . . I did terrible things. But now I can't remember what . . . And I just want to tell you . . . I hope you can forget, just as I've forgotten."

The words tugged at Tan's heart. They brought to mind the terrible fight in Switzerland when her mother had held a meat cleaver to her throat. But now Tan felt compassion. At the time, her mother had just lost her son and husband to brain tumors. "You're in a strange country with no support system, you don't speak the language, your kids are out of control, it seems like you're cursed," Tan says.

Despite the occasional moments of remorse, Daisy Tan seemed happier than she had ever been. She spoke as if her husband and son were not dead. Her memories brightened, sometimes taking the form of fairytale-like dreams.

One day Daisy Tan shared a new version of how she had met John Tan. "You with me," she said to her daughter. "We in elevator. All of a sudden, door open. You push me out and there you daddy on a dance floor waiting. You smiling whole time, tell me go see, go dance. Then you get back in elevator, go up. Very tricky, you."

Daisy Tan had magically included her daughter in a joyful memory. Amy saw how, in a sad way, the disease had been a gift. It seemed to erase much of her mother's sadness.

After her mother's death, Amy Tan rewrote her novel from start to finish. *The Bonesetter's Daughter* became the tale of a Chinese American woman's relationship with her mother as she was dying of Alzheimer's. The main character's mother has been both her adversary and her dearest friend.

The history between Tan and her mother had been a burden—and a gift. "What I know about myself," Tan has said, "is related to what I know about her, including her secrets."

Amy Tan is in a rock-and-roll band called *Rock Bottom Remainders.* The musicians in the band are writers, including Matt Groening, Stephen King (pictured with Tan), and Dave Berry.

Amy Tan has written six novels and won numerous awards. She has said, "I think books were my salvation; they saved me from being miserable."

Amy Tan

Born:

> February 19, 1952, in Oakland, California

Education:

> San Jose State University

Grew up:

> Various parts of northern California

Website:

> www.amytan.net

Favorite books:

> *The Catcher in the Rye*, J. D. Salinger
> *The House of Spirits*, Isabel Allende
> *Jane Eyre*, Charlotte Brontë
> *Lolita*, Vladimir Nabokov
> *Love Medicine*, Louise Erdrich
> *Love in the Time of Cholera*, Gabriel García Márquez
> *The Woman Warrior*, Maxine Hong Kingston

Author of:

> *The Bonesetter's Daughter*
> *The Hundred Secret Senses*
> *The Joy Luck Club*
> *The Kitchen God's Wife*
> *The Moon Lady* (for children)
> *The Opposite of Fate: A Book of Musings*
> *Sagwa, The Chinese Siamese Cat* (for children)
> *Saving Fish from Drowning*

A Conversation with Author
Gaiutra Bahadur

Q *How did you research this book?*

A I read *Dreams from My Father*, President Obama's memoir about growing up biracial and his search for his roots, which he wrote before he became a politician. I read a collection of autobiographical essays by Amy Tan, *The Opposite of Fate*. I also listened to, watched, and read interviews with each of them. It was very important for me to hear them tell their own stories in their own words.

Q *Both Obama and Tan went through a process of defining themselves through their writing. How were their processes similar?*

A Both of them had a hard time figuring out how to make two worlds fit: black and white for Obama, Chinese and American for Tan. For both of them, the problem seemed connected to a parent. By writing, Tan and Obama were able to explore their complex emotions about that parent. Words helped them make sense of their confusion and, as a result, helped them put their cultural conflicts in perspective, too.

Q *How was that process of defining themselves different?*

A Each of them had a difficult parent at the heart of their identity crisis. But they were difficult in almost opposite ways. Obama's father was not present enough in his life, while Tan's mother seemed to be way too present. Tan wrote fiction to come to terms with her mother and her culture. She could let her imagination fill in the gaps where secrets and mysteries were. Obama, by choosing to write nonfiction, couldn't do the same thing. He had to confront the secrets head-on, without protection.

Q *At the center of each story was a journey—Obama's to Kenya and Tan's to China. What role did these countries play in their stories?*

A It's a funny thing to feel that a place you've never seen has shaped your life—and even made it more difficult. Because Obama's father was born and raised in Kenya, and Tan's mother in China, both places became large and full of meaning in their children's imaginations. Obama and Tan saw these two countries as the source of their confusion about themselves. They also looked to them as the source of answers to their confusion.

Q *Both Tan and Obama struggled to define what it meant to be American. As an immigrant, did you identify with that struggle?*

A Yes, I did. I was almost seven years old when my family immigrated to America. I grew up feeling almost cut in half by the front door of our house. Inside was the Old Country—in our case, Guyana—with its customs and its accents. Outside was America—where people spoke in different accents and had different values. I have to say I felt like I didn't fit in either world. Growing up has meant figuring out a way to define myself and fit in both worlds.

Q *Obama wrote nonfiction and Tan, fiction. Do think there was a significant difference in the creative process they each went through?*

A Each form of writing presents its own challenges. I think nonfiction writers have to struggle more with their consciences, because they can sometimes harm other people by telling the truth. Even if the person is dead, as Barack Obama Sr. is, a reputation can be damaged. To write the best book you can, you have to be emotionally honest—but that can have its costs when real people are involved. I imagine that writing fiction may have freed Tan, allowing her to explore subjects she might not have been able to if she was writing nonfiction.

Q *In your experience, does travel to unfamiliar places often lead to new understandings of oneself?*

A Yes, it does. I'm never so fully aware of just how American I am as when I travel outside the United States. Everything you take for granted here—knowing how to greet people, how to dress, how to relate to strangers or friends of the opposite sex, what time to arrive or expect people to arrive for appointments—all of that has to be relearned when you're in another society. In learning how they do things, you figure out how you're most comfortable and happy doing things.

Q *These stories are also about learning to accept parents who are less than perfect. How did both Tan and Obama manage to achieve that acceptance?*

A They both managed to accept their parents in part by treating them as characters in a book. To understand a character, you have to think through his or her motives and background: Where did they come from? What happened to them to make them act the way they do? The best novels make us empathize with their main characters, even the most complicated and flawed ones. That process must have helped Obama and Tan reach a better understanding of their parents.

What to Read Next

Good Reads

Fiction

The Absolutely True Diary of a Part-Time Indian,
Sherman Alexie. (288 pages) *Based on the author's own
experiences, this book describes a quest to balance life in two
different worlds.*

American Born Chinese, Gene Luen Yang. (240 pages)
*The three stories in this graphic novel center on race, identity, and
acceptance.*

April and the Dragon Lady, Lensey Namioka. (214 pages)
*April, a 16-year-old Asian American, struggles to find her place in
the world, helped—or hindered—by her cunning old grandmother.*

Bud, Not Buddy, Christopher Paul Curtis. (272 pages)
*Ten-year-old Bud escapes from foster care and sets out on a journey
to find the father he never knew.*

Dragonwings, Laurence Yep. (256 pages) *This is the story of a
Chinese father and his son in San Francisco in the early 1900s.*

The Girl Who Fell from the Sky, Heidi W. Durrow. (272
pages) *The heroine of this story searches for her own identity after
the death of her mixed-race parents.*

Nonfiction

What Are You? Voices of Mixed-Race Young People,
edited by Pearl Fuyo Gaskins. (288 pages) *Young adults from
a wide mix of cultures share their experiences of growing up in the
United States.*

**Half and Half: Writers on Growing Up Biracial and
Bicultural,** edited by Claudine C. O'Hearn. (288 pages)
*Eighteen writers tell their stories of growing up and defining
themselves on their own terms.*

Books

The Joy Luck Club, Amy Tan. (288 pages) *Tan's first novel weaves together the stories of four Chinese American women and their Chinese-born mothers.*

Dreams from My Father: A Story of Race and Inheritance, Barack Obama. (464 pages) *In this memoir, Obama narrates his journey from childhood to adulthood and his path to self-discovery.*

The Woman Warrior: Memoirs of a Girlhood Among Ghosts, Maxine Hong Kingston. (209 pages) *One of Amy Tan's major influences, this book combines Chinese storytelling with the alienation and confusion Kingston felt in America.*

Films and Videos

NBC News Presents: Yes We Can! The Barack Obama Story (2009). *This program covers the life of Barack Obama from his early childhood through his inauguration as president.*

The Joy Luck Club (1993). *Amy Tan was one of the scriptwriters of this award-winning film based on her novel.*

To Live (1994). *This award-winning Chinese film tells the story of a husband and wife during and after the Chinese civil war.*

Senator Obama Goes to Africa (2007). *Obama narrates this movie about his visit to Kenya and other African nations.*

Websites

www.artandwriting.org
This is the website for the Alliance for Young Artists and Writers. Here you can find all kinds of advice, news about upcoming contests, and a wide selection of past works.

Glossary

adultery (uh-DUL-tuh-ree) *noun* a physical relationship between a married person and someone who is not that person's wife or husband

Alzheimer's disease (AWLTZ-hye-muhrz duh-ZEEZ) *noun* a disease of the nervous system that damages brain cells, making it increasingly hard to remember, to speak, and eventually to move

cannibal (KAN-uh-buhl) *noun* a person who eats other humans

communist (KOM-yuh-nist) *noun* a person who believes that all property should belong to the government or community to be shared by all

concubine (kon-KYOO-bine) *noun* a woman who is formally paired with a man but whose social status is below that of a wife

economist (ee-KON-i-mist) *noun* a person who studies the way money, goods, and services are created and used in a society

fishmonger (FISH-mun-guhr) *noun* a person who sells fish

gallant (GAL-uhnt) *adjective* brave, fearless, and courteous

heritage (HER-uh-tij) *noun* valuable or important traditions handed down from generation to generation

impersonate (im-PUR-suh-nate) *verb* to pretend to be someone else

memoir (MEM-wahr) *noun* a written account of the author's experiences

millet (MIL-it) *noun* a grain that is grown in dry climates for its small, edible seeds

mistress (MISS-triss) *noun* a woman who has an affair with a married man

monk (MUHNGK) *noun* a man who lives in a religious community and devotes his life to his god or gods

nationalist (NASH-uh-nuh-list) *noun* a person who fights for the independence of his or her country

opium (OH-pee-uhm) *noun* an addictive drug processed from the juice of unripe opium poppies

pall (PAWL) *noun* a feeling of gloom and sadness

panhandler (PAN-hand-luhr) *noun* someone who stops people on the street and asks for money or food

pen name (PEN NAYM) *noun* a made-up name used by an author instead of his or her real name

pre-med (PREE-med) *noun* college work that a student completes before going to medical school

relevant (REL-uh-vuhnt) *adjective* directly concerned with what is being discussed or dealt with

remainders (ri-MAYN-durz) *noun* books that are offered at a greatly reduced price because of poor sales

superstitious (soo-pur-STI-shuhs) *adjective* believing in magic, luck, or supernatural events

theme (THEEM) *noun* the main subject of a piece of writing

Sources

A FATHER'S SECRETS

Dreams from My Father: A Story of Race and Inheritance, Barack Obama. New York: Three Rivers Press, 1995. (including quotes on pages 4, 15–16, 26, 30–31, 34, 35, 39, 57)

"Acceptance Speech in Chicago as the President-Elect," Barack Obama. November 5, 2008.

"Barack Obama '83: Is He the New Face of the Democratic Party?" Shira Boss-Bicak. *Columbia University Today,* January 2005. (including quote on page 32)

"A Biracial Candidate Walks His Own Fine Line," Janny Scott. *New York Times,* December 29, 2007.

The Bridge: The Life and Rise of Barack Obama, David Remnick. New York: Knopf, 2010. (including quote on page 34)

"The Candidate: How the Son of Kenyan Economist Became an Illinois Everyman," William Finnegan. *New Yorker,* May 31, 2004.

"The Conciliator: Where Is Barack Obama Coming From?" Larissa MacFarquhar. *New Yorker,* May 7, 2007.

"From Books, New President Found Voice," Michiko Kakutani. *New York Times,* January 18, 2009.

"Homelands," David Remnick. *New Yorker,* January 12, 2009.

"Interview with Barack Obama," Connie Martinson. *Connie Martinson Talks Books,* August 1995. (including quote on page 17)

"A Law Review Breakthrough," Linda Matchan. *Boston Globe,* February 15, 1990. (including quote on page 34)

"Mau Mau Case: UK Government Cannot Be Held Liable." *BBC News,* April 7, 2011.

"Obama's Organizing Years, Guiding Others and Finding Himself," Serge Kovaleski. *New York Times,* July 7, 2008.

"Obama's Young Mother Abroad," Janny Scott. *New York Times,* April 20, 2011. (including quote on page 18)

"Postcard from Kogelo," Alex Perry. *Time,* November 5, 2008. (including quote on page 38)

"A Promise of Redemption," Paul Watkins. *New York Times Book Review,* August 6, 1995.

"The 'Rat-Ballers:' Obama's High School Crew," Neal Karlinsky and Dan Morris. *ABC News,* April 26, 2007. (including quote on page 30)

The Scramble for Africa, Thomas Pakenham. New York: Avon Books, 1991.

"Speech at the Boston Democratic National Convention," Barack Obama. July 27, 2004. (including quotes on pages 52–53, 55)

"The Story of Obama, Written by Obama," Janny Scott. *New York Times*, May 18, 2008.

"Talk About *Dreams from My Father* at Barnes and Noble," Barack Obama. November 23, 2004.

A MOTHER'S GHOSTS

The Opposite of Fate: A Book of Musings, Amy Tan. New York: G.P. Putnam's Sons, 2003. (including quotes on pages 62, 63, 67, 68, 75, 76, 91, 93, 95, 97–98)

"American Woman," Penelope Rowlands. *Mother Jones*, July/August 1989.

Amy Tan: Author and Storyteller, Natalie M. Rosinsky. Bloomington, MN: Compass Point Books, 2006.

"Amy Tan's Style and Her Other Works." The Big Read: National Endowment for the Arts.

"A Bond of Unbroken Silence, Illness, and Death," Sean Hubler. *Los Angeles Times*, February 13, 2001.

"Daughter of Time," Jane Ganahl. *San Francisco Chronicle*, February 4, 2001.

"How Stories Written for Mother Became Amy Tan's Best Seller," Julie Lew. *New York Times*, July 4, 1989. (including quote on page 5)

"Interviews with Amy Tan," Jami Edwards. BookReporter.com, February/March 2001.

The Joy Luck Club, Amy Tan. New York: Penguin Books, 1989. (including quote on page 88)

"A Life on the Brink," Alison Singh Gee. *People*, May 7, 2001.

"A Life Stranger than Fiction," Helena de Bertodano. *Daily Telegraph*, November 11, 2003. (including quote on page 96)

"Mother of *Joy Luck Club* Author Amy Tan Is Dead," Jonathan Curiel. *San Francisco Chronicle*, November 24, 1999. (including quote on page 70)

"Mother Tongue," Amy Tan. *Threepenny Review*, 1990. (including quote on page 87)

"Striking Cultural Sparks," Elaine Woo. *Los Angeles Times*, March 12, 1989.

"Tan's Books Excavate Life's Joys and Pains," Deirdre Donahue. *USA Today*, February 19, 2001.

"A Uniquely Personal Storyteller," Academy of Achievement interview with Amy Tan. June 28, 1996. (including quotes on pages 60, 68, 78, 80, 85, 100)

Index